Amazon Tap

Amazon Tap For Beginners

Everything You Need To Know About Amazon Tap Now

Table Of Contents

Introduction

In this book, you will find all the information you need about Amazon Tap. You get to earn all the ins and outs of using its many features- from using it for streaming your favorite tracks to getting traffic updates.

Bluetooth, Wi-Fi, voice-enabled speakers are increasingly becoming popular in recent months. These speakers offer more than just crisp, rich, full-range sounds to every user. Amazon took speakers to a whole new level though by incorporating the amazing app called Alexa. Now, Amazon Speakers can do more than just stream music.

With Alexa, Amazon Tap can be used to listen to audiobooks and podcasts. You can also use it to get information like the weather, sports updates and traffic. By just pressing a button, you can also ask Alexa to organize stuff like set up alarms and timers, manage your schedule (with Google Calendar), and create shopping lists.

Alexa is basically an artificial intelligence or a virtual assistant. Users can talk to her to ask her to do something or to ask for specific information.

This is not an entirely new concept. There are already other virtual assistants like Siri, Google Now, Watson and Cortana. If so, then what makes Alexa- and Amazon Tap- different and worth your money?

That and all your other questions will be answered in this comprehensive book.

Let's begin the journey.

Chapter 1: Getting to Know Your Amazon Tap

Amazon Tap is the latest addition to Amazon speakers. It gives you full-range sound that is rich and crisp every time. Connect Tap to Alexa and you can do so much more, like manage schedule, get updates on weather and news, manage your Smart Home devices and of course, control playback as you listen to your favorite music.

Amazon Speakers

Amazon Tap is one of the Alexa-enabled speakers offered by Amazon. It has pretty much the same abilities and functions as Amazon Echo and Amazon Echo Dot. Its main difference from the other 2 is that it is portable. Echo and Echo Dot need to be continually connected to a power source in order to function, and that means there are certain limitations to its use inside the house or room. You can bring Amazon Tap with you and use it as a regular speaker. If you have a mobile hotspot, you can still use its Alexa capabilities on-the-go.

While all Amazon Speakers (Echo, Echo Dot and Tap) are all voice-enabled, Tap has a **Talk** button that you need to press once in order to activate Alexa and make requests or ask questions. With Echo and Echo Dot, all you have to do is to say Alexa's name and straightaway give a request or ask a question. Echo and Echo Dot need to be continually connected to a power source because of this. Tap is portable and does not have to be continually plugged into a power source. It has batteries that can be recharged. In order to conserve battery life, Tap will have to be "awakened" by pressing the **Talk** button before you can use it as a Bluetooth or Wi-Fi-enable speaker or to access Alexa.

The need for pressing the **Talk** button is the major let-down of Tap but there is a very good reason for this. It has to conserve battery life. Users of Echo and Echo Dot get to enjoy hands-free multitasking with Alexa. However, the use of these devices is limited indoors. You may have to press the **Talk** button to access Alexa but Tap's portability means you can do more outdoors.

You can spend a nice and relaxing day at the beach with music blaring from your Tap. Turn on your mobile hotspot and you can have pizza delivered to you right where you are.

You may also use Tap in your car to listen to Flash Briefing. Take mere seconds to press the **Talk** button and ask Alexa about traffic conditions to avoid getting caught in traffic. You can't do that with hands-free Echo and Echo Dot. What's a small move of pressing a button if you can enjoy Alexa and her multifarious skills anywhere you go? Then again, you will have to have a mobile hotspot to access Alexa on-the-go.

The great experience does not stop there. Even with indoor use, Tap is still fun to use. You can easily carry it anywhere in the house (or backyard) with you. With Echo and Echo Dot, you can't always enjoy its superior sound. These 2 speakers do come with a voice remote, allowing you to still give voice commands to Alexa even if you are out of range of the speakers' built-in microphone. Voice remote is not needed with Tap because you can carry the entire speaker with you.

Amazon Tap Sound Quality

Amazon Tap is portable, smaller than Echo and Echo Dot. However, sound quality is crisp and excellent. The speakers inside the device are stereo, like the one in Echo Dot. Tap comes with Dolby-poweredaudio, giving you excellent sound quality. When you stream music in Tap, you get 360-degree sound, thanks to its 2 1.5-inch drivers. Its dual passive radiators provide a little bit of bass, which improves sound quality.

Audio input is Bluetooth-supported. Tap, unfortunately, does not support Bluetooth Audio.

Tap also supports AUX Audio Input, which Echo and Echo Dot do not. It does not have any support for AUX Audio Output.

Voice remote is a feature that users enjoy with Echo and Echo Dot. With Amazon Tap, there is no support for Voice Remote.

Amazon Tap Hardware

Gaining an understanding of the hardware of Amazon Tap is the first step to understanding how the whole thing works. This device is a portable speaker that is both Wi-Fi and Bluetooth enabled. It basically works by connecting to the Alexa Voice Service. It is a speaker that can play music and do so much more like provide information such as the weather, sports update (such as team scores and game results), and news in an instant.

General Appearance

Tap is so much smaller than Echo. Tap is portable but not pocket-sized. This latest Amazon speaker dimensions are 1159 mm x 66 mm x 66 mm (6.2" x 2.6" x 2.6"). That's roughly about the size of a large drinking glass. It weighs 470 grams- a little more than 1 pound, making it an easy tote.

It is cylindrical in form, which makes it a comfortable fit in your palm when you carry it. It only comes in black color. However, you get to choose from 5 different bright hues with the optional Sling.

The Sling is a silicone cover (selling for $19.99 on Amazon) you slide over the Tap to protect it from the elements. The 5 colors to choose from include blue, black, white, tangerine and magenta.

The Sling has a small, built-in hook that you can use to hang the Tap. You will have to remove the Sling when you charge the Tap in its charging cradle. If you do not want to remove the Sling, use the mini-USB charging cable instead to charge your Tap.

The Front and Top Controls

Talk Button

Look at Amazon Tap at the front and see the prominent single large button. This is the Talk button. This is also known as the Microphone button.

Pressing this button activates Alexa. Once pressed, the user to speak and give commands to Alexa.

Look at the top of the speaker and these buttons are present:

Playback controls

Play/Pause button

- Middle button
- Press to either play or to pause music currently playing on the speaker

Previous/Next

- 2 buttons, one arrow facing to the left (Previous) and one arrow facing to the right (Next)

Volume Down/Volume Up

- 2 buttons, one arrow pointing upwards (volume up) and the other arrow on the opposite end facing down (volume down)

Front light indicators

-   These light indicators give information on Amazon Tap's current status.
-

<u>Light indicator behaviors and what they mean</u>

-   If blue light is pulsing over the cyan lights in a left to right direction, Amazon Tap is starting up. This light indicator behavior happens after the Power button is pressed then held for a few seconds.
-   If the light strip is filled with all cyan lights, Amazon Tap is waiting for you to talk to her or to ask her a question. This light indicator behavior happens after the Talk (Microphone) button is pressed.
-   If all the cyan lights are pulsing quickly, Alexa is responding to your recent request.
-   If the amber light is quickly pulsing in a left-to-right direction, Amazon Tap is in the setup mode. This indicates that you can use Alexa app for connecting Amazon Tap to Wi-Fi.
-   If blue lights are pulsing over the unlit lights, Amazon Tap is entering the Bluetooth pairing mode.
-   If red lights are pulsing, an error occurred and Alexa cannot complete the request. An example for this light indicator behavior is when Wi-Fi network went down before Alexa could complete the request.

Back controls

Turn the speaker around and see the following buttons at the lower portion:

Power button

- Topmost of the column of buttons at the lower portion at the back of Amazon Tap speaker
- To turn on and off, press and hold the Power button
- The ring around the Power button glows if the device is on
- The Power button is not lit if the device is turned off
- Pressing but not holding the Power button will put the device in sleep mode, to conserve battery life

3.5 mm Audio Port

- The next button directly below the Power button
- Compatible devices are connected to Amazon Tap via this port
- To connect, use the auxiliary audio cable (available as a separate purchase)
- After the compatible device is connected, user can listen to media and music saved on the device
- This only supports line-in connections
- While a device is connected to this port, interaction with Alexa is not possible; device must be disconnected first before interacting with Alexa

Micro USB port

- The third item in the column, which is an outlet with tiny pins to receive the micro USB
- This port is primarily for charging the Amazon Tap with the micro-USB charging cable and the power adapter (comes with the speaker upon purchase)

Bluetooth/Wi-Fi port

- This is the last button in the column
- Has the standard Bluetooth sign
- Press to enter the Bluetooth or Wi-Fi setup mode
- For Wi-Fi setup mode, press and hold this button for 5 seconds
- For Bluetooth setup mode, press the button once but do not hold
-

Power and Cables

Power adapter

- Connect this to the charging cable and plug into a power outlet

Charging cradle

- Has 2 small pins where Tap will connect in order to charge
- Disc-shaped
- Neat and low-profile

Micro-USB cable

- Use only this when charging your Tap

Chapter 2: Setting up Amazon Tap

To start using Amazon Tap, set it up first. Follow these simple step-by-step guides to help you in setting up the entire device and a few key features.

Setting up Amazon Tap

Before you can use Amazon Tap, you have to set it up first by downloading the Alexa app. Once downloaded, you can set up the device and stat talking to Alexa. Without the app, you won't be able to manage music, shopping lists, alarms and other features of Amazon Tap.

Alexa is support by any device that has the following operating systems:

- iOS 7.0 or higher
- Android 4.0 or higher
- Fire OS 2.0 or higher

Note that the 1st and 2nd generations of Kindle Fire tablets have no support for Alexa app.

1. Download Alexa
   - Access the app store in your device and type "Alexa app" in the search bar,
   - Open the app and type "Alexa app" in the search bar. Then click on the icon of the app. Select the "Install" button to start the download.
2. Turn Amazon Tap on.
   - Connect the power adapter to the charging cable.
   - Connect the charging cable to the charging cradle.
   - Place Amazon Tap into the charging cradle.
   - Plug the adapter into a power (electrical) outlet.
   - The speaker's front light indicators should turn blue then orange.

- Alexa will greet you.
- Amazon Tap is now in the setup mode.
3. Connect to a Wi-Fi network.
    - Once the app is downloaded, there is a set of instructions that will guide you in connecting to a Wi-Fi network.
    - In case this process does not automatically happen, look for the Wi-Fi/Bluetooth button. Press and hold this button for 5 seconds to enter the setup mode.
    - Once in the setup mode, open Alexa app.
    - Choose **Settings**.
    - Choose the option **Set up a new device**
4. Talking to Alexa.
    - After you have successfully set up Alexa, the Amazon Tap is now ready to be used.
    - If you wish to talk to Alexa, locate the **Talk** (**Microphone**) button.
    - Speak using short and natural phrases.
    - After talking to Alexa, put the speaker into sleep mode by pressing (but not holding) the Power button. This will conserve battery life.

Chapter 3: Amazon Basics

After downloading Alexa and setting up Amazon Tap, your next step is to learn the basic power up activities.

Charging the Amazon Tap

The normal charging time of Amazon Tap is less than 4 hours. With a fully charged battery, the speaker can be used for continuous play back of up to 9 hours. If the speaker is on higher volume settings, playback time is shorter because of the higher demand on the battery.

You can charge Amazon Tap by either using the Charging Cradle or directly connecting to a power outlet.

- If you will use the Charging Cradle, place Amazon Tao into the appropriate dock.
- Connect the micro USB cable into the port in the Charging Cradle.
- Connect the power adapter to the other end of the charging cable.
- Plug into a power outlet.

Alternatively, you can directly plug the micro USB cable into the port at the back of Amazon Tap. Connect the other end to the power adapter and plug into a power outlet.

Important Note:

Always use the power adapter that comes with your Amazon Tap. Using other power adapters will lengthen the charging time.

Also, charge your Amazon Tap using the Charging Cradle or the micro USB cable connected to the power adapter. Never charge the speaker in a computer's micro USB port.

- Amazon Tap is charging when you see that the Power button is glowing.
- You can check the current charge or battery level while Amazon Tap is charging via Alexa.
  - o Talk to Alexa and simply ask her, "How much battery is left?"
  - o Use your downloaded Alexa app to check the charging status by accessing **Settings** menu and look at the information provided.
  - o Check battery status using Amazon Tap's playback controls. Locate the buttons for **Volume Up** and **Volume Down**. Press and hold these buttons at the same time. The information on the current battery charge percentage will be given by Alexa.

Amazon Tap Sleep and Power Modes

You can put Amazon Tap in the sleep mode to conserve battery charge, and then power it up again, ready for use anytime.

- Turn Amazon Tap on
  Locate the Power button. Press and hold for a few seconds (1-5 seconds) until you see that the button starts to glow. This indicates that the speaker is on.
- Turn Amazon Tap off
  Press and hold the speaker's Power button until a tone is heard. This indicates that Amazon Tap has turned off. Check that the Power button is also unlit when the speaker is off.

- Place Amazon Tap in sleep mode
  Press but do not hold the Power button. You should not hear any tone but the Power button should be unlit. Sleep mode reduces battery consumption to conserve battery charge but will enable you to resume speaker functions quickly.

Chapter 4: Basic Connectivity

Connectivity is among the top features of Amazon Tap. It has a Bluetooth-enabled speaker you can use to stream audio files from your tablet or phone. In order to do that, you must first pair Amazon Tap with your mobile device.

Pairing Amazon Tap with your mobile device

You must first pair Amazon Tap with your mobile device before you can start streaming audio from a tablet or phone. To do this, activate the Bluetooth pairing mode of your mobile device. Amazon Tap and the mobile device must be in close range. Wait for the mobile device to detect Amazon Tap before you can successfully pair.

While paired, Alexa will not be receiving any phone calls, text messages and other notifications. Alexa will also not be able to read these texts and notifications from the mobile device. These are kept separate. In addition, you can't send audio files from Amazon Tap to any Bluetooth headphones or speakers.

To pair Amazon Tap and your mobile device:

1. Locate the **Wi-Fi/Bluetooth** button. You will find this at the back portion of Amazon Tap, bottommost portion of a line of buttons and ports. Press this button but do not hold. If you want to exit the pairing mode, press this button again once.

2. Alexa will notify you when Amazon Tap is ready for pairing with a Bluetooth device.
3. On your mobile device, open the settings menu for Bluetooth.
4. Choose the name of your Amazon Tap and wait for a connection to be established.
5. Alexa will notify you if the pairing was successful.
6. Once paired, your mobile device can now stream audio to Amazon Tap.
7. You can disconnect your Amazon Tap from your mobile device, by pressing the **Power** button only once.

Once you have paired Amazon Tap to your mobile device, connection is automatically established once Bluetooth is turned on. You do not have to keep pairing every time. If you want to connect again, press the **Microphone/Talk** button on Amazon Tap. Talk to Alexa and say "Connect". Your mobile device will then automatically connect to Amazon Tap. In case you have paired Amazon Tap to multiple Bluetooth devices, the last device paired will be the one it will connect to.

Connecting Amazon Tap to a Wi-Fi network

You can also connect via Wi-Fi network to stream audio, speak to Alexa, and process commands.

Amazon Tap can connect to both private and public Wi-Fi networks. The Wi-Fi frequency bandwidth supported is 2.4 GHz only. Amazon Tap can also connect over mobile hotspots with 802.11b/g/n standard.

Make sure that your Amazon Tap is charged. Turn on your Amazon Tap and open the Alexa app in your mobile device.

1. Open the home screen of Alexa app.
2. Open the navigation panel at the left.
3. Select the option **Settings**.
4. From the menu that appears, tap on the name of your Amazon Tap.
5. Choose the option **Update Wi-Fi** from the menu window that opens. If this is the first time your device (Amazon Tap) is connecting to Wi-Fi, then choose the option **Set up a new device** instead.
6. Next, press and hold the button for Bluetooth and Wi-Fi, located at the back of the speaker. Keep holding the button until the light indicators are glowing with orange light.
7. Look at the Alexa app open in your mobile device. As Alexa connects to your Amazon Tap, a list of available Wi-Fi networks will be available.
8. Select your preferred Wi-Fi network. Alexa may ask you to manually connect to the network. For this, go to your Wi-Fi device settings.
9. Select your Wi-Fi network.
10. A prompt may appear, requiring you to enter the password (if password enabled). If not, then the device will automatically try to establish a connection.

   a. In case your Wi-Fi network's name is not in the list, scroll down the list and look for the option **Add a Network**. This is for hidden Wi-Fi networks, a possible reason for not seeing your Wi-Fi network name in the list. You may also choose the option **Rescan**. It may be that your Wi-Fi network was missed the first time your device scanned.
   b. If you are required to manually add your Amazon Tap to your Wi-Fi router's list of devices approved to connect with, just scroll down the screen (where the prompt to enter the Amazon Tap name) until you see your Mac address.

c. You may also save your password for your Wi-Fi network to Amazon. This way, you will not always have to re-enter the Wi-Fi network password every time you connect. Just tap on the checkbox for this option to save your password. Once saved, it will be remembered even if you switch to a different Wi-Fi network. You will not be required to re-enter it if you use this saved Wi-Fi network again.

d. You are not allowed to save on Amazon any information entered if you are using a public network connection. Any information entered for public networks requiring web browsers to sign in like a room number, or a pre-shared password can't be saved to Amazon.

11. Click **Connect** once the Amazon Tap and the Wi-Fi network has established a connection.

12. When you receive a confirmation message in the Alexa app, you can now start using Amazon Tap and its many features that involve Alexa.

Saving Passwords on Amazon

Saving your password to Amazon is one convenient feature. Amazon can configure compatible devices for you. This way, you will no longer have to re-enter passwords every time you open your Tap and connect to the Wi-Fi network and to Alexa. Amazon will configure your other compatible device so you won't have to repeat the process.

Security and privacy are guaranteed. When you save your Wi-Fi password/s, it will be sent through a secured connection. The password/s will then be stored in an Amazon server as an encrypted file. The saved password/s will only be used by Amazon to connect and configure your own compatible devices. Amazon will not share the information to any third party if you do not give the permission to do so.

If you do not want to save your Wi-Fi password/s to Amazon, it's totally fine. You do not have to save if you do not wish. When you connect your Tap to your Wi-Fi network, you have the option not to save your password.

In case you have changed your password/s, you should save it again in Amazon. You have to re-run your compatible devices through the Wi-Fi setup process. Next, reconnect these devices to your Wi-Fi network and then save the new password again in Amazon. It is essentially repeating the process, as if saving the Wi-Fi network and the password for the first time.

Connecting Amazon Tap with Wi-Fi Hotspots

Some mobile devices can be used as a mobile hotspot. You can connect Amazon Tap to this in order to use Alexa and stream media or audio files. This feature further makes Amazon Tap a great on-the-go speaker device.

You must have Amazon Tap's latest software update. Your Amazon Tap software should be at least 120005720 or higher.

The Alexa app should be downloaded in a supported mobile device. Examples include mobile devices with Android or iOS operating systems. Your phone (mobile device) should also have the capability to be a Wi-Fi hotspot.

Before you can connect to a Wi-Fi hotspot for the first time, the option for this kind of connection may not present. The problem may be from the software currently used by your Amazon Tap. It may be outdated and cannot support connectivity with a mobile hotspot. In this case, follow these steps:

- Connect Amazon Tap first to a home Wi-Fi network.
- Find an available downloadable copy of updated software for your device that can support connectivity features with a mobile hotspot.

- Download the latest software. Follow the instructions on installing the updated software in your device.

Once your device is now capable to support this connectivity feature, you can now proceed to setting up Amazon Tap to be able to connect to a Wi-Fi hotspot.

1. Open the settings menu of your mobile device.
2. Turn on your Wi-Fi hotspot by tapping the option for this feature.
3. Take note of the password and the network name of your mobile hotspot.
4. Open your downloaded Alexa app. Open the navigation panel at the left and tap **Settings**.
5. Touch to select the name of your Amazon Tap.
6. Select the **Update Wi-Fi** from the menu options.
7. Next, prepare your Amazon Tap for connection by pressing and holding the **Wi-Fi/Bluetooth** button for about 5 seconds, until the light indicators glow in orange light. Amazon Tap is now connecting to the Wi-Fi hotspot.
8. You will now see a list of Wi-Fi networks available near the device. You can see this list in the Alexa app open in your mobile device.
9. Tap the name of your mobile hotspot.
10. Alexa might ask you to enter the password or to connect manually. Just open your mobile hotspot device's settings menu and tap perform these commands:
    a. Scroll down the opened menu settings.
    b. Look for and tap the option **Use this device as a Wi-Fi hotspot**.
    c. Tap the option **Start**.
    d. A prompt requiring the name of the network and password of the hotspot will appear. Fill in the required fields with the information called for.
    e. After entering all the required information, tap the button **Connect**. All the information must be correct, including capitalized letters, if any. Amazon Tap will not be able to successfully connect if any of the

entered information is incorrect. Even the slightest error like a capitalized letter when it should be in small caps will invalidate the information.

f. Turn on the Wi-Fi hotspot by activating it in the phone settings.

g. Wait for Amazon Tap to detect your Wi-Fi hotspot and will attempt to connect.

h. If Amazon Tap is able to connect o your mobile hotspot, Alexa will notify you and send a confirmation of the successful connection.

Do note that Amazon Tap will be using your mobile device's data connection. This will incur data charges. Be sure to monitor data connection usage while Amazon Tap is connected to your mobile hotspot to avoid surprises when your phone bill arrives. It is also prudent to talk to a representative of your service provider to clarify data charges and other information regarding the use of mobile hotspot.

Alexa Software Updates

The latest software at this time of writing is 150003820. This update has new and enhanced features, with bug fixes to improve performance. Alexa app is continuously evolving to match the changing needs and wants of users. It is also constantly improving in order to provide a more enjoyable and satisfying experience. Getting the latest version is also a good way to get the most out of your Tap, taking your Amazon Tap experience to new heights.

To check the software you currently have:

1. Open your downloaded Alexa app in your mobile device.
2. Tap on the left navigation panel to open the menu.
3. Select the option **Settings**.
4. Tap on the name of your device.
5. A list of options will open.
6. Scroll down this menu and look for the option **Device software version**.

Check if your app software version is the latest. If not, then you can download the latest version for your Amazon Tap:

1. Turn your Tap on.
2. Make sure you have an active Wi-Fi connection and your Tap is connected to it.
3. Do not say anything into your Tap to avoid any interference.
4. You will notice that the light indicators glow in blue light when an update is ready for installation.
5. Your Tap will automatically install the latest software update. Installing may take up to 15 minute. Speed of installation depends on how strong and fast your Wi-Fi connection is.
6. If you have trouble with updating your Tap, restart it. After restarting, wait for Tap to try to update its software again.

Chapter 5: Amazon Tap and Media Streaming

Amazon Tap is basically a speaker where you can play music. You may also use Tap to stream media like audiobooks and podcasts. Tap also allows you to upload your music collections from Google Play Music, iTunes, etc. to Amazon and stream it.

The list of both subscription-based and free streaming services supported by Alexa is continually growing. You can stream music and media with your Tap from the following streaming services:

- Prime Music
- Amazon Music
- Spotify Premium
- TuneIn
- Audible
- iHeartRadio
- Pandora

Alexa can stream music, live radio, podcasts, audiobooks and more in your Tap from these streaming services. You can automatically access music from the Amazon Library once you have registered your Tap in your Amazon account.You also have automatic access to the numerous audiobooks that are available in the Audible library. Members of Amazon Prime can also stream music and media with Prime Music stations, playlists and songs.

Listening to Prime Music

Prime Music has quite a huge selection of music from different artists. Hundreds of new ones have been recently added. Songs by artists like Maroon 5, Katy Perry, Drake, The Weeknd, Ariana Grande and Lady Gaga are all available from streaming in your Tap. Prime Music gives you access to a comprehensive catalog. You can stream unlimited songs from various albums, stations and playlists all for free.

To start streaming:

1. Open your Tap and make sure it is connected to a Wi-Fi network or a mobile hotspot.
2. Press the **Talk** button and say, "Alexa, play (name of artist/song/playlist/Prime Station)."

You can get access to Prime Playlists, too. These are hand-crafted song collections from the catalog in Prime Music. There are over 1 million songs to choose from at no additional cost for eligible US Amazon Prime members.

Prime Stations available are free of ads, so you do not experience any unnecessary interruption while listening. Streaming music stations are personalized and offer continuous song playback straight from Prime Music catalog. You can dislike or like songs on Prime Station. You may also skip songs as you like.

To control playback in Prime Music, press the **Talk** button once and ask Alexa to do things like:

Alexa, play relaxing sounds from Prime Music.

Alexa, play songs from Prime Music.

Alexa, play dance songs from Prime Music.

Alexa, play Icona Pop music.

Alexa, play the playlist "Sunny Day Classical".

Alexa, play "music from Santana.

Alexa, play jazz music from Prime Music.

Alexa, play Jason Mraz Prime Station.

Alexa, play "Classical Focus" Prime Station.

The latest in Prime Music is the Fab Four. Yes, well-loved tracks by the Beatles are now available in Prime Music Stream. Selected Beatles' tracks available include Lucy in the Sky With Diamonds", "Let It Be", "A Hard Day's Night" and "Yesterday".

To listen to Beatles' tracks, press the **Talk** button and speak into Tap, saying:

"Alexa, play (title of Beatles' song)."

Third-Party Music Services

Other third-party music services like SpotifyPremium, Pandora and iHeartRadio will require you to link your subscription or existing account to your Amazon account or Alexa.

To link to a music service:

1. Open the Alexa app and click the menu icon at the left navigation panel.
2. Click the option **Music & Books**.
3. Select the name of the music streaming service you have an existing account or subscription with.
4. Choose the option **Link account to Alexa**.
5. A sign-in page will appear.
6. Sign in by entering the email account and the password you have for that streaming service, not for your Amazon account.
7. If an error message appears, reset the password and username for that music streaming service.Then try to link that account again to Alexa.
8. If you want to unlink you subscription from Alexa, you can by opening Alexa, perform steps 2 and 3, then choose the option **Unlink account from Alexa**.

You need to connect Tap to a Wi-Fi network or mobile hotspot if you wish to play music from a music streaming service to your Tap. However, you may still stream music saved in your devices like tablets and phones through Bluetooth

Streaming Media and Music over Bluetooth

Amazon Tap supports A2DP or Advanced Audio Distribution Profile. This allows for streaming audio files via Bluetooth connection. Tap also supports AVRCP or Audio/Video Remote Control Profile. This profile enables users to operate connected mobile devices through voice control.

Controlling media playback while on Bluetooth connection

Pair your mobile device with Tap then open your favorite media app such as Spotify. Press the Play button. Next, press the **Talk** button on your Tap and tell Alexa:

Alexa, pair Bluetooth" or "Alexa, pair my device

You will then be able to play your music over Tap. Voice controls you can use include these sample hands-free voice control requests:

Alexa, play

Alexa, pause

Alexa, restart

Alexa, resume

Alexa, stop

Alexa, next

Alexa, previous

Alexa, connect my tablet (or phone)

Alexa, disconnect my tablet (or phone)

If you request Alexa to play specific albums, songs, playlists or artists, Tap will pausethe music playback on your mobile device. Music available on your Amazon Music library will be played instead. If you want to play music on your Tap over Bluetooth again, press the **Talk** button and say, "Alexa, connect." Then press the Play button on your mobile device where the music will be playing from.

You may use voice commands to control the music playing over your Tap. Try these commands by pressing the **Talk** button on your Tap then say any of these:

Alexa, turn it up.

Alexa, volume 7

Alexa, next song

Alexa, stop the music

Alexa, Alexa, softer

Alexa, what's playing?

Alexa, mute

Alexa, loop

Alexa, set the sleep timer after 1 hour

Alexa, stop the music after 30 minutes

Alexa, cancel sleep timer

Besides these, you may also ask Alexa these requests:

(while Prime Music is currently playing)

Alexa, add this song

(while listening to the radio or a music sample is currently playing)

Alexa, buy this album (or song)

You may also give your ratings or reviews to a song currently playing with these requests:

(while a track or song is playing from Prime Stations/iHeartRadio/Pandora)

Alexa, I like this track

Alexa, thumbs down

Uploading Music

You can also upload music on your Tap from Google Play, iTunes and similar services. Music library on your Mac and/or PC can also be uploaded on Amazon Music and be streamed into your Tap. Once uploaded to Amazon, you can now tell Alexa to play these songs. You also get to have playback controls using voice commands like "Next", "Stop" and "Previous".

Amazon allows you to upload a maximum of 250 songs free of charge. Songs you purchased from Amazon's Digital Music Store are not included in the 250-count. If you want to upload more songs, you can avail of Amazon Music subscription. With the subscription, you can upload songs of up to 250, 000.

Changing to Amazon Music Subscription

To change from free Amazon Music to Amazon Music Subscription:

1. Open the page for Amazon Music Settings.
2. Select a subscription.
3. Choose the option **Upgrade music library storage**.
4. Check the option for your preferred payment method.
5. Select **Continue**.
6. Once you have upgraded your subscription, you will immediately have access to a bigger storage.
7. You have the option to disable the auto-renew option. If you disable this, you will still be able to use the current storage capacity until the end of the current billing cycle.

Connecting audio devices with Amazon Tap

You may also stream audio file to Amazon Tap without having to connect via Bluetooth or Wi-Fi. You can connect an audio device directly to Amazon Tap via an audio cable.

Examples of audio devices you can connect to this speaker include an MP3 player, a tablet or a smartphone. Any audio cable that has a standard 3.5mm jack can be used to connect audio devices to Amazon Tap.

Amazon Tap cannot be used for any audio-out connections to other devices and/or to other speakers. It also does not support the use of headphones.

Once you plug the audio device, Alexa is automatically disabled by Amazon Tap. This will allow you to directly stream music without any interruption.

To start streaming, simply plug one end of the audio cable into the appropriate port in the audio device. Insert the other end into Amazon Tap's 3.5mm audio input port. This port is right under the speaker's **Power** button.

Discovering and Purchasing Music

If you want to search for or buy music, you can easily do so with Alexa. Talk to Alexa and search for songs and albums available on the Digital Music Store.

> *Alexa, sample songs from Katy Perry.*
>
> *Alexa, what song is popular from Regina Spektor?*
>
> *Alexa, play sample songs by the Beatles.*
>
> *Alexa, buy "Walking with a Ghost" by Tegan and Sara.*
>
> *Alexa, shop for new music by the Weeknd.*

You can listen to a sample of the music first before making a purchase. Once you like a music sample, you can tell Alexa to purchase it for you. You simply tell her, "Alexa, buy this song (or album)".

31

Purchases you made in the Digital Music Store will automatically be stored in your own Amazon Music Library. This storage feature is free. These purchases are not counted to your storage limits, as mentioned earlier. That means even if you already have full storage of 250 songs in your library, you do not have to upgrade your storage to accommodate Digital Music Store purchases. Music purchased in the Store is also available for download or playback on compatible devices, including Amazon Tap. This is as long as the device/s is/are registered on your Amazon account.

If you are a Prime member, you can just add Prime Music to your library without paying extra charge.

Chapter 6: Quick Fix Guide

You might find a few issues while using Amazon Tap. Most of these issues are not serious can be quickly fixed.

Amazon Tap is not connecting to a Wi-Fi network

Amazon Tap does not support peer-to-peer or ad-hoc networks. Check that you are trying to connect to a Wi-Fi network, not to Wi-Fi direct, peer-to-peer network connection. This device connects to Wi-Fi networks with 2.4 GHz, using the standard 802.11 b/g/n.

In case your device does not connect to a Wi-Fi network after you have already set up Amazon Tap with Alexa, try these quick-fix tips:

- Try to reconnect to the Wi-Fi network.
- Check that the password of the Wi-Fi network has not been reset. Look at the icon next to the name of the available Wi-Fi network. If a Lock icon is found, then you will have to connect to that network and enter the correct password.

This password is different from the password you use for your Amazon account.

- Check if other devices can connect to the Wi-Fi network you are trying to connect to. Try connecting to that network using other gadgets like tablets or phones. If these other gadgets can connect to the network, the problem is not with the network. If other devices cannot connect also, then the problem is with the network. Contact the network administrator, the person that set up the network or the internet service provider for assistance.
- Update your modem or router hardware's firmware.
- You may use the Amazon account password to connect if you have saved the Wi-Fi password to Amazon. Your Amazon Tap may not be connecting to Wi-Fi if you recently changed your password. Just re-enter the new Wi-Fi password and connect again.

Decongest Wi-Fi connection

Inconsistency in your Wi-Fi connection can affect the performance of Alexa and Amazon Tap. This is often among the most common reasons for Amazon Tap not connecting to a Wi-Fi network. The inconsistency is often related to Wi-Fi congestion. Multiple devices connected all at the same time will compete for the network services. You have to reduce congestion to improve performance.

- Turn off the Wi-Fi connection of other devices that are not really in use to free up a few more bandwidth on the network.
- Move Amazon Tap closer to the modem and router. It is possible that objects and walls are getting in the way of good and consistent reception.
- Place your Amazon Tap in an area away from possible signal interferences like baby monitors or microwave ovens.

Restart network hardware and Amazon tap

If Amazon Tap is not connecting to Wi-Fi, try restarting both the device and the network hardware. Most issues involving intermittent Wi-Fi and connection issues can be solved by restarting the device, the router and the internet modem.

- Turn off the modem and the router. Wait for 30 seconds.
- Turn the modem on, waiting for it to restart.
- After restarting the modem, turn the router on. Wait for the router to restart.
- While the hardware restarts, restart the Amazon Tap. Press and then hold Amazon Tap's Power button until it dims (hold for about 5 seconds). Once the button is dim, press it again to restart the speaker.
- Retry connecting to the Wi-Fi network.

If none of these steps resolves connection problems, you will have to contact your network administrator, router manufacturer, or Internet service provider.

Amazon Tap is not charging

Before you do anything else with your device, you have to remember these things to avoid damage to the device and have charging problems:

- Always use the micro USB cable and the power adapter that came with Amazon Tap.
- When you charge Amazon Tap, always from the charging cradle or from a power outlet. Expect longer charging time when charging from a computer's USB port.
- Make sure that all connections are secure. The micro USB cable should be securely connected to the power adapter and to the charging cable or to the micro USB port at the back of Amazon Tap.

- Check that the Power button on Amazon Tap is glowing when charging. The Power button will not glow immediately upon charging if the battery was completely drained. Amazon Tap will have to charge for a few minutes before the Power button lights while charging.

Check the device's charging cradle

The problem might be on the connection to the charging cradle, if you are using this to charge your Amazon Tap.

- Check the connections. Nothing should be in the way between Amazon Tap and the charging cradle.
- Remove the micro USB connected to the charging then reconnect. The connections should be secure. Loose connections are not allowing a continuous flow of electricity to charge your Amazon Tap.

Check the device's power adapter

1. Remove the micro USB cable from the charging cradle.
2. Plug this cable to the micro USB port at the back of Amazon Tap.
3. Disconnect the charging cable and the micro USB cable.
4. Connect the micro USB cable directly into the micro USB port at the back of your Amazon Tap device.
5. Connect the power adapter and plug directly into a power outlet.
6. If Amazon Tap light indicator does not light up to show that the device is charging, disconnect the micro USB from the speaker. Turn off the device by pressing and holding the Power button until you can hear a tone.
7. Turn the device on again by pressing and holding the Power button until it glows.
8. After the device has restarted, connect the micro USB cable again. Plug the power adapter to a power outlet.

9. Charge the device for at least 1 hour.

Reset Amazon Tap

Resetting the device is done if it remains unresponsive to quick fixes. You can resort to this step if trouble persists with your Amazon Tap. However, it is still better to restart your device and see if the problem persists. Reserve resetting if all other maneuvers prove futile.

Resetting is also an option if you want to remove all the changes you have made to Amazon Tap settings. After you have reset this device, you will need to register once again to an Amazon account. You also need to re-enter device settings before you can use Amazon Tap again.

To reset, follow these simple steps:

1. Locate the **Previous** button (located at the playback controls on top of Amazon Tap). This is the arrow that facing towards the left.
2. Next, locate the **Wi-Fi/Bluetooth** button.
3. Press then hold both **Previous** and **Wi-Fi/Bluetooth** button for 12 seconds.
4. Observe the light indicators on Amazon Tap as you hold these 2 buttons. The lights should turn orange and then change to blue. Keep holding the 2 buttons.
5. Wait until the light indicators will turn off then on again.
6. When the lights turn on, it should be orange. This indicates that the device is now in the setup mode.
7. Get your device where you have downloaded Alexa.
8. Open Alexa app and connect to a Wi-Fi network.
9. Register again to an Amazon account.

Alexa does not understand your request

You can talk to Alexa and obtain information such as the weather, sports scores and time. Alexa understands standard English phrases and will respond appropriately. In case talking to Alexa does not yield any result, it does not mean there is a problem with the app or the device. The solution may be as simple as checking connectivity.

Alexa can only work if there is a continuous, stable Wi-Fi connection. Otherwise, Alexa cannot function. An active, stable Wi-Fi connection allows Alexa to stream music from cloud storage. Alexa can also stream other media stored from the cloud. The app can also answer any of your questions. You can also give Alexa a specific request and this will be carried accordingly.

If Alexa does not respond to requests, try these steps:

Move Alexa to an ideal location

Unresponsiveness may be due to poor connection or interference. Check that your Alexa device, in this case your Amazon Tap, is away from any interfering devices like baby monitors and microwave ovens.

Amazon Tap should also be at least 8 inches away from the walls. These objects may be getting in the way of communication between Alexa and Amazon Tap or Alexa and the Wi-Fi connection.

Check that Amazon Tap is not out of range. The signal may not be reaching your device. Place Amazon Tap to a higher location. Avoid placing the device on the floor, as this may be too low for the signal to reach.

Speak clearly

When you speak to Alexa, make sure that there is no background noise. This can confuse Alexa and lead to misunderstanding. Alexa is designed to respond only to clear and unambiguous requests. If Alexa detects several phrases, words or sounds all at once, the app is designed to make no move to respond to it.

When you talk to Alexa, you should speak clearly and naturally. Again, if Alexa cannot understand your words, the app will not respond.

Request should be specific

If Alexa gets confused, no response to the request will be made. Make sure that your request is specific.

- If Alexa does not respond, repeat your request.
- Your request may be too general and Alexa is not sure what you actually mean. For example, you are asking for the weather in Springfield. There are numerous cities all over the world that bear that name. Alexa will not give you the weather for all these cities. Again, the app requires one request and it should be specific. Your request should be "Alexa, what is the weather in Springfield, Illinois?" That is a more specific request than simply asking Alexa "What is the weather in Springfield?"
- To make sure that Alexa heard your request right, the app has a record of what request was heard (received). To check, follow these steps:
    - On your phone (where Alexa is downloaded), go to the home screen.
    - Select the option **More**. This is at the bottom of the screen's interaction card.
    - You will be given access to the list of requests that Alexa heard. Check which request was not responded to and see if Alexa heard you right. There is also an

option where you can listen to a record of the request that was made. You can also see the feedback. Tis way, you make the appropriate adjustments when you repeat the request.

o If not, then restate that request and be clear and specific.

Voice Training

Amazon Tap has a feature called Voice Training. This allows you to be able to train Alexa to adjust and understand you specific speech patterns and voice tone. Alexa app will show 25 different phrases that you will have to read during Voice Training. You will speak these phrases into your device where Alexa app is downloaded. The app will then record, analyze, and make adjustments according to your speech patterns. This process will improve Alexa's capability to recognize your speech and to respond more appropriately to your questions and requests.

The Voice Training feature is only available on Amazon Tap and on Echo devices.

When you are using Voice Training, you will be required to read aloud the 25 different phrases in the app. Say these phrases into your Tap during the entire process. So before you start, make sure you press that **Talk** button once. Alexa will still be able to process the phrases even if you do not finish speaking all the phrases.

To get the best results, you should say the phrase using your normal voice into Tap.

To start Voice Training:

1. Get your mobile device and open the downloaded Alexa app.

2. Open the menu by tapping the left navigation panel.

3. From the menu that opens, select the option **Settings**.

4. Choose the option **Voice Training**.

5. Choose the option **Start Session**.

6. Press the **Talk** button on your Tap.

7. Say the sample phrases that appear on the app.

8. Select the option **Next** after speaking the phrases.

9. If you want to repeat the phrase, press **Pause** in the app then select **Repeat Phrase**.

10. At the end of your Voice Training session, choose the option **Complete**.

11. If you want to end your session before finishing all the phrases, press the option **Pause**, then **End session**.

Fixing Bluetooth Issues

If your Amazon Tap is not connecting to the mobile device where Alexa app via Bluetooth, check that it has support for the different Bluetooth profiles. Alexa can connect over Bluetooth with Amazon Tap, as well as Echo and Echo Dot. These devices support the following Bluetooth profiles:

- A2DP SNK
  This stands for Advanced Audio Distribution Profile. This Bluetooth profile allows for streaming audio from a mobile device like tablet or phone to the Alexa device like your Amazon Tap.
- AVRCP
  This stands for Audio/Video Remote Control Profile. This Bluetooth profile allows for a hands-free voice control as long as the mobile device (with the downloaded Alexa app) is connected to the Amazon Tap.

Bluetooth connection problems with Alexa usually stem from incompatibilities.

If compatibility is not the issue, try these solutions to fix Bluetooth connectivity issues.

Check batteries on the Bluetooth device

- Check that the batteries are working in your Bluetooth device. Check that the non-removable battery is fully charged.
- If the Bluetooth device has removable batteries, try replacing it with new ones and check if connectivity improves.

Check for the presence of any interference

Bluetooth issues may stem from interference in the connection between the Bluetooth device and your Amazon Tap.

- Transfer both Amazon Tap and Bluetooth device away from any possible source of interference. Check that the area is not near other wireless devices, baby monitors and microwave devices.
- Move the Bluetooth device near Amazon Tap when you are trying to connect. Bluetooth connectivity is dependent on distance. If the device is far from Amazon Tap, connection will be difficult to establish.

Clear all the Bluetooth devices

Too many connected devices can interfere with establishing a stable Bluetooth connection. There will be a lot of devices competing to make a connection. These other options will keep propping up, attempting to make a connection. To clear, follow these steps:

- Open Alexa on the device where you have downloaded the app.

- Tap on the menu that will open the navigation panel on the left.
- Select the option **Settings**.
- Select the name of your Amazon Tap device.
- Tap the option **Bluetooth**.
- Select the option **Clear**.

After all the devices have been cleared, restart your Bluetooth device. Restart Amazon Tap also and then try to make a Bluetooth connection.

Pair the Bluetooth devices

After resetting, both the Bluetooth device and Amazon Tap, pair them again.

1. Open the menu settings in your mobile device.
2. Turn on the Bluetooth.
3. Make sure that Amazon Tap is also nearby.
4. Talk to Alexa and say "Pair".
5. Alexa will enter the pairing mode.
6. Wait for the name of your Amazon Tap to be detected by your mobile device.
7. Once Amazon Tap has been detected, tap its name in your mobile device.
8. Wait for a few seconds as your devices pair.
9. Alexa will notify you if a successful connection was established.

Chapter 7: Getting to Know Alexa

Alexa is a voice-activated computing app. In the case of Amazon Tap, you have to press the Talk button first to wake up Alexa. This is unlike Amazon speakers like Echo and Echo Dot where merely saying "Alexa" already activates the app.

If you ask Alexa a question or make a specific request, the app will provide an answer or a result. This much very similar to how other virtual assistants function. What sets Alexa apart is that it is centralized and functions are dedicated to in-home Amazon devices.

Alexa cannot do everything like Ironman's Jarvis can. While the app may be limited in this comparison, Alexa does offer a wide range of interesting skills. You can ask the app about the weather, traffic, sports update, news, movie show times, calendar events and so much more. With Alexa, your Tap becomes your window to a lot more things beyond merely being a speaker for listening to music.

With Alexa downloaded in your mobile device, you can have so much fun with it. You can access Alexa by talking via the **Microphone/Talk** button in the Tap. You do not have to press and hold this button as you make requests. Just press once and talk. Alexa will continue to listen up until you have finished speaking.

Enabling Alexa skills

Before you can start using Alexa skills, you have to enable it first. These skills are voice-driven capabilities allowing you to request Alexa to perform certain functions or gather certain information for you. These skills enhance Alexa's capabilities and help you do more with your Amazon Tap and similar devices (i.e., Echo and Echo Dot).

When you want something, you do not have to call on your phone to order or to search the web for team statistics. All you have to do is to tap the **Talk** button and say your request.

Before you speak your request into the Tap, you must first enable the skill in the app. Then, you can make your voice requests based on the sample request phrases for that skill as shown in the app.

There are 2 ways to enable an Alexa skill. If you already know the skill, then simply tap the **Talk** button in your Tap and say "Enable (the name of the skill) skill". If not, you can manually enable the skill right in the Alexa app.

1. Get your mobile device where you have downloaded the Alexa app.
2. Open the app.
3. Look for the left navigation panel and tap it.
4. From the menu that opens, choose the option **Skills**.
5. You will see a list of skills categories. Browse through these skill or type the skill you want in the search bar (at the top of the list of categories).
6. Right beside the skill name is a button **Enable Skill**. Tap this option if you want that skill to be enabled.
7. Once enabled, you can use that Alexa skill on your Tap.

You can ask Alexa (by pressing the **Talk** button on your Tap once and speaking into it) to open and use that skill. For example, you have enabled the Capital One skill. With this, you can check your credit and other information about your Capital One account. To open and use it, press the **Talk** button on your Tap and say, "Alexa, open Capital One skill".

If you want to learn more about the skill, you can make a request to Alexa to open the detail page for that specific skill. You can look at the skill's detail page by opening the app and going to the skill that you want to learn more about. Alternatively, you can talk to Alexa to know more about the skill. Press the **Talk** button on your Tap and say, "Alexa, Capital One help".

When you do not want to use an enabled Alexa skill anymore, disable it. You can open the app and manually disable the skill/s. you may also talk to Alexa to request the skill to be disabled. Press the **Talk** button and say, "Disable (name of the skill) skill".

How Alexa Skills are processed

When you speak into Tap and say your request, your words are streamed into a cloud service dedicated to Alexa. The app will recognize your speech and then processes it, attempting to determine what you want. After processing, Alexa will send a structured request to the specific skill you have requested. The result will then be sent to you.

To illustrate: Say you ordered pizza through Alexa with the request "Alexa, order a 10-inch Domino's pepperoni pizza." Alexa will process this request and determine what you meant by this. Then, the information will be sent to the appropriate skill. In this case, send the information to a nearby Domino's to place the order.

All of these processes, from speech recognition to conversion, are handled by the app in the cloud.

Interacting with the Alexa app

All the abilities of Alexa can be utilized through a basic process. First, you wake up Alexa by pressing the **Talk/Microphone** button. Then, ask a question or make a request. The basic format is this:

> *"Alexa, (question)"*

> e.g. *"Alexa, what is the weather in Chicago today?"*

Alexa will process this and extract information from the cloud that will answer your question. Once information is obtained, Alexa answers:

"Right now in Chicago, there are clear skies."

For requests:

"Alexa, (request)"

e.g.*"Alexa, get high for Chesapeake Bay from Tide Pooler."*

Alexa will process this request and determine what you wish to obtain. The app will then send the request for this specific information to Tide Pooler. Then, when the information is given, the response you will receive is:

"Thursday July 28th in Chesapeake Bay, the first high tide will occur around 12:38 in the morning and will peak at around 8 feet...."

You may also use Alexa skills to control smart home devices. The device must be cloud-controlled and connected to the Internet, like through a smart home hub.

For example, you wish to adjust the lights in the living room. That light must be cloud controlled and currently connected to the Internet. The lights in the living room must have been previously configured and given that name, then saved to Alexa. Then you can say:

Alexa, dim the living room lights.

Setting your device location

Some Alexa skills will need to have your device location in order to provide better service and information that is more accurate. Examples of skills that will require your location include those that provide information about the time, weather and local features such as local searches for restaurants and movie schedules.

You can change the default location in your Tap by:

1. Open Alexa menu by tapping the icon on the left navigation panel.
2. Choose **Settings**.
3. Select the name of your Tap.
4. Choose the section **Device location**.
5. Select the option **Edit**.
6. You will be asked to enter your complete address. Fill in the fields for the street name, the city, the state and the ZIP code. This detailed address is needed so that Alexa can give you the most accurate and most relevant information.
7. Tap the **Save** option once you have provided the complete address.

Chapter 8: Alexa Native Capabilities to Try on your Tap

Alexa has quite an impressive list of native skills. These are skills readily available upon download.

Calendar

Alexa can read, add and give you updates on events you have on your Google Calendar. Alexa is also able to tell you about the events in shared calendars.

You must first enable Calendar in your Alexa settings:

1. Open the Alexa app.
2. Tap the **Settings**.
3. Select the option **Calendar**.

Next, link your Google account to Alexa:

1. Open menu at the left navigation panel of the Alexa app.

2. Choose **Settings**.

3. Select **Calendar**.

4. Choose **Google Calendar**.

5. Choose **Link Google Calendar account**.

6. You will be prompted to sign in to your Google account. Enter your Google email and your password for this account.

If you do not have any Google account, create one at http://calendar.google.com.

You can request Alexa to give you updates on your schedule by simply pressing the **Talk** button on your Tap once and ask:

(for information on your next event)

Alexa, what is on my calendar?

Alexa, when is my next event?

(for specific information on an event happening on a particular day and/or time)

Alexa, what is on my calendar on Thursday at 10 AM?

Alexa, what is on my calendar tonight?

You can add events to your calendar by just speaking to Alexa. For example, you are out in the park and you came across someone. You both agreed to meet for lunch next week. You can place this event in your calendar immediately before you forget it by talking to Alexa.

To add events, try these sample requests:

Alexa, add event to my calendar.

Alexa, add '10 AM meeting with Mr. Tanner on July 16th at his office' to my calendar.

Alexa, add 'brunch meeting at Lilly's next Tuesday' to my calendar.

You must have a Wi-Fi network connection or you have a mobile hotspot with you so you can connect to Alexa. This makes it easier and more convenient for you to keep track of and manage your schedule.

Anyone else who is part of your Amazon Household can also have access to your calendar, as you also have access to theirs. Events contained in your accounts that you linked to Alexa will be available to anyone who uses your device.

Setting up timers and alarms

Alexacan be requested to set up multiple timers and alarms by simply talking to her.The volume of these timers and alarms are independent of the rest of Tap's other sound settings. You can have a very loud volume setting for an alarm but your playback volume is soft.

To set the volume of your timers and alarms:

- Open Alexa.

- Open the **Settings** menu.

- Select the name of your Tap.

- Choose the option **Sounds**.

- Choose the option **Alarm and Timer Volume**.

To set up an alarm or a timer, press the **Talk** button on your Tap and say clear request like these ones:

Alexa, wake me up at 5 in the morning.

Alexa, set the alarm for 8 AM.

Alexa, set the timer for 25 minutes.

Alexa, what time is it?

Alexa, how many minutes left in my timer?

Alexa, what is the date?

Alexa, cancel the alarm for tomorrow at 6 AM.

Alexa, what are my timers?

Alexa, what alarms were set for next week?

Alexa, cancel the timer for 35 minutes.

Alexa, stop (when an alarm goes off)

Alexa, snooze (when an alarm is set up with multiple timers)

Setting repeating alarms

Aside from managing your schedule and adding events with Alexa via your Tap, you can also set up repeating alarms. Alexa can wake you up every day or remind of your daily tasks every day or on the same day every week. You can also set up an alarm for weekdays and set up a separate one for the weekends.

To set up an alarm:

Alexa, set a repeating alarm for weekdays at 6:30 AM.

Alexa, set an alarm for every Thursday at 4PM.

If you want to edit your alarms, you can do so in the Alexa app. Open Alexa, go to the settings and look for Alarms.

Finding local restaurants and businesses

Alexa can find local restaurants and establishments for you using your device location. You have to turn this on and enter your exact address for this skill.

This app can help you find establishments in your locality. All you have to do is to ask Alexa, like in these sample requests:

Alexa, what Indian restaurants are nearby?

Alexa, where are the most popular diners in the area?

Alexa, what bakeries are in the area?

Alexa, what are the top-rated restaurants nearby?

Alexa, give me the address of the closest pharmacy.

Alexa, where is the nearest hardware store?

Alexa, find the phone number of the nearest police station.

Alexa, find the address of the nearest clinic.

Alexa, find the phone number of a nearby mechanic.

Alexa, find the hours of a nearby pharmacy.

Things to Try

This skill will give you daily updates and tips about Alexa. You will receive more helpful tips on how to get more out of Alexa as part of your daily Flash Briefing.

To enable this skill, open your Alexa app. From the settings, choose Flash Briefing from the list of skills. Add the option **Alexa Things to Try**

Movie show times

Alexa continually grows and expands the many skills and capabilities to make your life easier. Now, you can use your Tap and ask Alexa the show times of movies in theaters within your area. Alexa can help you plan your next movie date by giving you information on what films will play in theaters and what time these movies start.

To get this type of information, just ask:

(For movies playing in nearby theaters)

Alexa, what movies are playing this weekend?

(For movie genres playing in theaters nearby)

Alexa, what romantic movies are playing on Friday night?

(For specific show time schedules in your area)

Alexa, when is 'Finding Dory' playing?

Alexa, what time is 'Ghostbusters' playing?

Alexa, what movies are playing between 6 PM and 10 PM?

(For additional information such as ratings)

Alexa, tell me about the movie "Star Trek Beyond"?

Alexa, what movies will be playing at the (theater name) on (day/s)?

(For movies in theaters outside your locality/in another city)

Alexa, what movies are playing this weekend in (city)?

Alexa, when is (movie title) playing in (city) at the (theater name)?

By enabling this skill, Alexa can give you updated information on what is playing in theaters within your area or even in another city. You just have to place your address in the settings in the Alexa app.

Information from IMDb is accessed by Alexa to find the movies and the theaters where these are playing. Alexa also provides additional information such as ratings, based on IMDb information also.

Getting traffic information

Want to find the quickest route to your office and avoid traffic on Main Street? Want to know the traffic situation in the downtown area? Alexa can help you.

You should first open this skill in the app and enter your point of origin then your destination. After this, you can now ask Alexa about the traffic situation within this route.

Alexa, what is the traffic condition right now along 5th Street?

Alexa, what is my commute?

Getting weather updates

Alexa can also give you updates on the weather in your area and elsewhere in the world. You can get information about international, national and local weather forecasts.

Make sure that your device location is updated for this skill to function better. You may request weather conditions by tapping thee **Talk** button once in your Tap and ask Alexa, such as these sample requests and questions:

Alexa, what is the weather forecast today?

Alexa, what is the weather in Chicago today?

Alexa, what is the weather forecast at the beach tomorrow?

Alexa, will it snow tomorrow?

Alexa, what is the weather in Miami on Saturday?

Alexa,, what will be the weather in Washington DC tomorrow?

Alexa, what is the weather in Toronto this weekend?

Alexa, tell me the extended forecast in San Diego, California.

Alexa, is it going to be sunny on Monday?

Learning about the latest Sports update

Sports fans love this feature. You can ask Alexafor scores of finished games or even the live scores of ongoing games. You can also ask Alexa for the game schedules of your favorite team.

Alexa's supported leagues include the following:

- NBA
- NFL
- MLB
- NCAA
- MLS
- WNBA
- NHL
- NCAA FBS Football
- NCAA men's basketball
- English Premier League

To get your daily dose of sports update, press the **Talk** button on your Tap and ask Alexa, like these sample question:

Alexa, how are the Oregon Ducks doing?

Alexa, who is winning the current NBA game?

Alexa, did the Milwaukee Bucks win?

Alexa, when will Chelsea play next?

Alexa, what is the latest score in the Chicago Bulls game?

Alexa, who won in the Ohio State Buckeyes football game?

Alexa, who is winning in the Seattle Storm game?

Alexa, what is the score in the Washington Nationals game?

Alexa, how are the Kentucky Wildcats doing?

Managing To-do and Shopping lists

With your Tap and Alexa, you can easily manage your lists of things to do and things to buy. You can easily keep track of your future purchases as well as upcoming tracks.

For this skill, press the **Talk** button and ask Alexa for stuff like these:

Alexa, add milk to my shopping list.

Alexa, create a To-do list.

Alexa, what is on my Shopping list for next week?

Alexa, what is on my to-do list for today?

Alexa, add engine check-up on my to-do list for Friday.

Ordering products from Amazon

You may use Tap to make purchases in Amazon, as long as you are a member of Amazon Prime. With Alexa, you can order selected Prime-eligible items. To access this capability, you need to have an Amazon Prime membership. A 30-day free trial membership or an annual one is accepted. You must also have a US billing address. You should also have a 1-Click payment method.

When you order through Alexa via your Tap, the app will use the default payment and the shipping address available in your 1-Click settings. Orders for physical products in Amazon are eligible for free returns.

To purchase an item categorized as Prime-eligible, get your Tap and press the **Microphone (Talk)** button and say:

> *Alexa, order* (name of Prime-eligible item)

When Alexa has already found the product you asked, you will be required to confirm the order. Answer with either "Yes" or "No" into the Tap.

If you want to re-order an item, press the **Talk** button and speak to Alexa:

> *Alexa, reorder* (name of item)

After Alexa has found the item you requested, you will have to confirm the purchase by telling Alexa "Yes" or "No".

If you want to add a particular item to your Amazon cart, press the **Talk** button and say:

> *Add* (name of item) *to my cart*

You also have an option of cancelling an order right after you have confirmed its purchase. Press the **Talk** button and say:

Cancel my order.

In case Alexa cannot cancel your order, log into your Amazon account and manage your orders in **Your Orders**.

Basic requirements for making purchases on Amazon through Alexa

In order for your purchases to be valid and completed, you need to complete a few requirements first.

- When buying music from Digital Music Store:
  - Payment method
  - US billing address
  - 1-Click payment method
- When purchasing physical products (Prime-enabled):
  - Payment method
  - US billing address
  - 1-Click payment method
  - 30-day free trial or annual Amazon Prime membership
- When adding products to Amazon shopping cart on the website:
  - Amazon account

- When tracking the shipping status of a recent order:

    o   Amazon account

Once you requested for search or purchase of an item on Amazon, Alexa will scan several options for purchase such as:

- Order history for Prime-eligible stuff

- Prime-eligible things available on Amazon

- Amazon's Choice (these are items that are well-priced and highly rated with Prime shipping)

The results of the search through these purchasing options will provided to you. Alexa will tell you if the item you requested is available, along with the name of the item (e.g., brand, model number, etc.) and its price. Alexa will then ask you to either cancel the order or to confirm the purchase.

If the item you requested is not available or for some reason Alexa cannot complete your purchase, you will be offered any of these options:

- You may add that item to your Amazon cart

- You may add that item to your Shopping List on Alexa

- You may get your mobile device and open the Alexa app to find more options on how to deal with this item

Alexa searches your order history to know what specific brand, model or type you usually buy. If your recent request is not found in your order history or if that item is already out of stock, Alexa will offer you an alternative.Alexa will browse through Amazon's Choice and pick the items with top rates, good prices and Prime shipping closest to your original item request. For example, you ordered a certain brand of paper towels. That item is out of stock.

Alexa will search through Amazon's Choice for a similar item and with price near the one you requested. Alexa will make this known to you, saying:

> "I didn't find that in your order history but Amazon's Choice for paper towels is (brand). The order total is (price). Should I order it?"

Once you have confirmed your purchase, Alexa will go ahead and finalize your purchase on Amazon. Alexa will use the default payment and the shipping settings that you have placed in your Amazon account.

You can also manage your settings for shopping on Amazon through Alexa app. You can choose to turn off the voice purchasing capabilities. There is also an option that you can enable, which will ask for a confirmation code for every order before a purchase can be completed.

There are some products that cannot be purchased using voice controls on your Tap. These physical products include:

- Apparel
- Jewelry
- Shoes
- Watches
- Prime Now
- Prime Pantry
- Amazon Fresh
- Add-On items

Tracking packages

Finalized Amazon purchases can easily track your package with the Alexa app. You can keep track of your package/s without using a computer or calling on your phone. Alexa can give you updates about your package- even tell you when it will be arriving. There's more-Alexa will even give you the date and time you placed that specific order. The app will also provide a link to your order and details about it.

To track or get updates on your orders, press the **Talk** button on your Tap and say:

Alexa, track my order.

Alexa, where are the things I ordered from Amazon?

In case that you have multiple open purchases, the purchase with the closest delivery date will be provided. You can also manage and track your purchases from **Your Orders** in the Alexa app if Alexa cannot track your order.

Listening to audiobooks

Audiobooks available on Kindle Unlimited or Audible can now be listened to in your Tap via Alexa.

To start listening, press Tap's **Talk** button and make requests like these to Alexa:

Alexa, play the book "To Kill a Mockingbird."

Alexa, pause.

Alexa, read "Bossypants" from Audible.

Alexa, read "Is Everyone Hanging Out Without Me?"

Alexa, go to chapter 5.

Alexa, resume my book.

Alexa, go back to chapter 1.

Alexa, go back.

Alexa, go forward.

Alexa, previous chapter.

Alexa, next chapter.

Alexa, set the sleep timer in 45 minutes.

Alexa, restart.

Alexa, cancel the sleep timer.

Alexa, stop reading in 20 minutes.

Reading Kindle books

Alexa can read Kindle books available in your library for you and you can listen to these through your Amazon Tap. Books Alexa can read to you include those you have bought from the Kindle Store, shared to you through the Family Library, or what you have borrowed from Kindle Unlimited or Kindle Owners' Lending Library. This skill uses the same text-to-speech technology currently being used in for news articles, calendar events and Wikipedia articles.

To make Alexa read your Kindle books, press **Talk** button on your Tap and say requests like:

Alexa, read (title of book on Kindle).

Alexa, read Kindle book.

Alexa, go forward.

Alexa, pause.

Alexa, go back.

Alexa, resume.

Chapter 9: Other Things to Try with Alexa

Aside from the basic or native Alexa skills, there are additional skills you can download or enable.Open the Alexa app and look for the menu of Alexa skills. Alexa app also displays what skills are currently trending and popular.

There are over 1,500 Alexa skills you can try and have fun with. These skills allow you to do a lot of things, from ordering a Domino's pizza to checking your credit card balance. To activate these skills, all you have to do is to talk to Alexa.

Some of these are third-party skills from big brands like Domino's and Uber. These additional skills expand what you can do with Alexa such as get a ride from Uberand manage your finances with Capital One. There are also smaller niche-utility skills available like skills for guitar-tuning and crafting reminders for Minecraft. Of course, fart-making noise skill is also available in Alexa.Several of the third-party skills available on Alexais related to controlling smart home devices.

Most of the time, if you want to use third-party skills, you will have to use "invocation words". These are words that tell Alexa the specific skill you want to use. For example, you want to order from Amazon using Alexa's Amazon ordering skills. Just say, *"Alexa, ask Fitbitabout my resting heart rate."*Or, *"Alexa, order a 10-inch pepperoni pizzafrom Domino's."*

Latest Alexa features

Alexa keeps up with its users. It keeps getting smarter and able to do more stuff for you. Here are the new skills you can enjoy with Alexa on your Amazon Tap:

Get *Game of Thrones* quotes and more

Game of Thrones fans will surely love this new skill. You can ask Alexa to give you quotes from the series. Alexa will even answer questions about the series. Simply ask Alexa, just like in these sample requests and questions:

> *Alexa, what are the words of House Stark?*

> *Alexa, give me one quote from DaenerysTargaryen.*

> *Alexa, who are the characters from The Westerlands?*

Flash Briefing

Flash Briefing can now be customized to provide updates on local news. Go to Alexa app in your mobile device. Open the settings and choose the major metropolitan news source that caters to your area. Set this as the source of your local news for Flash Briefing. Once set and activated, you can now request Alexa any time to give you your daily dose of local news.

You can have your local news via Flash Briefing by asking Alexa:

> *Alexa, what is my Flash Briefing?*

Alexa app will deliver you pre-recorded news updates from broadcasters like BBC News, the Economist and NPR. You also get the latest headlines from Associated Press. Weather information from AccuWeather is also made available to you when you enable the Flash Briefing skill in Alexa.

A card will appear in your Alexa app home screen after requesting for Flash Briefing. Tapping this card will give you access to numerous links of full stories of the different news and headlines. You can tap these links if you want to read more about that specific news or story.

To enable Flash Briefing, set up the settings in your Alexa app.

- Open the Alexa menu by tapping the icon on the left navigation panel.
- From the menu that opens, select the option **Settings**.
- Scroll to look for the option **Flash Briefing**. Tap this option.
- Next, you will be given a list of news headlines, weather updates and shows with switches adjacent to these. Flip the switches next to the updates you wish to receive in your Flash Briefing.

Once you have enabled Flash Briefing and enabled the updates you wish to receive, you can now use this amazing Alexa skill. Use these requests to obtain Flash Briefing:

- To listen to Flash Briefing:
  - Press the **Talk** button in your Tap.
  - Speak into your Tap and say, "Alexa, what is my Flash Briefing?"
  - To navigate the Flash Briefing as you listen to the contents, just say "Next", "Cancel" or "Previous".

PGA Tour

Alexa now has a new skill for PGA Tour. You can now track the activities, statistics and standings of your favorite golfers. You can also get the latest, to-the-minute information about a golfer's performance. The latest standings in the FedEx Cup is also available once this skill is enabled.

To enable the PGA Tour skill, open the Alexa app. Go to settings and enable this skill. Then, to get your latest dose of PGA, ask Alexa:

Alexa, ask PGA Tour for latest leaderboards.

Alexa, ask PGA Tour for Jordan Spieth statistics and standing.

Review and rate Alexa skills

Now, you can review Alexa skills and rate them. Alexa users can also share their experience with the different skills with other users. Users can see what other Alexa users are saying about these skills as well.

To review and rate the different Alexa skills:

1. Open Alexa app.
2. Tap icon to open the menu from the left navigation panel.
3. Select the option **Skills**.
4. Tap on any of the third-party skills available on Alexa that you want to review and give your own rating.
5. Next, scroll down the menu that opens and tap **Reviews**.
6. In the menu, choose the option **Write a Review**.
7. Enter your reviews and rates in the appropriate fields in the dialog box that opens.

Alarm Tones

Alexa offers several alarm tones for you to choose from. Recently, more than 10 new tones have been added. You can choose soothing tones such as Adrift. Upbeat, loud tones such as Pulsar are also available that will surely grab your attention when your alarm goes off.

To choose alarm tones, open the Alexa app. Then follow these steps:

1. Open the menu at the left navigation panel.
2. Choose the option **Alarms**.
3. Options on customizing the alarm settings will open.
4. Change the default tones for alarms to your desired one.
5. Once you have set it, you ask Alexa to use this as the alarm tone. To do this, press the **Talk** button in your Tap and say, "Alexa, set an alarm for 4 PM."

Search for restaurants and business

You may also ask Alexa to find nearby restaurants and businesses. Alexa provides these details from Yelp. Update your device location under the **Settings**of Alexa app menu.

Listening to Sports Update

With Alexa, you can listen to your Sports Update on your Amazon Tap any time. Sports Update can be customized to give you the latest about your favorite teams. By enabling this skill in your Alexa, you can have access to the latest schedules and games.

To customize Sports Update:

1. Open menu in Alexa app.
2. In the **Settings** menu, select **Sports Update**.
3. Next, add your favorite teams that you want to receive updates about.

You can now alsoAlexa to give you updates any time. Just make sure your Tap is connected to Wi-Fi. Press the button for **Talk** in your Tap and say, "Alexa, give me my Sports Update".

Home device control with Insteon

Now, you can use Insteon Hub with Alexa to control more home devices. Insteon is already compatible with a number of home devices so it will be easy to sync with Tap.

NCAA Football Schedules and Scores

Alexa now has a skill that will allow you to get the schedules and scores for NCAA FBS or the Division 1-A football games. As with the updates you get from NBA games, WNBA, NCAA men's basketball, NFL, NHL, MLS and MLB, you can receive scores (from completed games) and live scores. You can also ask Alexa to find out when is the next game of your favorite teams, e.g., "Alexa, when is Oregon Ducks' next game?"

The list of what Alexa can do continues to grow rapidly. This is largely to the open approach Amazon incorporated into the software that powers this app.

Chapter 10: Amazon Tap, Alexa and Smart Homes

Like Echo and Echo Dot, Tap can also be used to control your smart home devices. You can connect stuff in your home like the thermostat, fan, AC unit and lights- as long as these are SmartThings.

SmartThings are home devices that work with Amazon Tap, Echo and Echo Dot. These can connect with Alexa and be controlled using voice controls. SmartThings can be adjusted, turned on or turned off with just one voice command to Alexa.

Get Started

To start using your Tap to control SmartThings through Alexa, you have to purchase SmartThings first.

Then, you have to download the SmartThings app to your mobile device (phone, tablet, etc.).

Open the SmartThings app and create an account.

Next, set up your Amazon Tap and then download the Alexa app in your mobile device (phone, tablet, etc.).

Here is a list of all the smart home gadgets compatible with Alexa. This app can control these devices:

(Native support)

- Philips Hue LEDs (on and off, dimming only but no color changes possible)

- Lifx LEDs (on and off, dimming only but no color changes possible)

- BelkinWeMo Light Switches

- BelkinWeMo Switches

- Insteon Hub-connected devices (lights and switches)

- Wink Hub-connected devices (lights and switches)

- SmartThings Hub-connected devices (lights and switches)

- If This Then That (IFTTT)

- Emerson Sensi Wi-Fi Thermostat

- Ecobee3 Connected Thermostat

- Honeywell Lyric Connected Thermostat (coming soon)

- Nest Learning Thermostat

(Skill support)

- Lifx LEDs (with full color control capabilities)
- Automatic Labs Connected Driving Assistant
- Fitbit
- Skybell HD Video Doorbell
- Scout DIY Security
- Garageio
- HomeSeer Home Automation
- Vivint
- Stringify
- D-Link Wi-Fi Smart Plugs
- Rachio
- TP-Link Kasa
- Big Ass Fans Haiku Smart Ceiling Fans (coming soon)
- Ooma Smart Home Phone System
- Lutron Home Lighting Control Devices
- James Martin/CNET

Connect SmartThings

After downloading and setting up the devices, it's time to connect your SmartThings with Tap and Alexa.

Start with your Alexa app in your mobile device.

1. Open the app.
2. Open the menu on the left navigation panel. This is the icon with 3 horizontal lines.
3. Select the option **Smart Home**.
4. Another menu will open. Scroll down to look for the option **Your Smart Home Skills**. Tap this option.
5. Another list of options will appear. Scroll down and select the option **Get More Smart Home Skills**.
6. In the search field that will appear, type "SmartThings".
7. Next, tap the button **Enable** to enable the SmartThings skill.
8. A dialog box will open, requiring you to enter your email address and password for SmartThings.
9. Enter the correct information in the required fields then select **Log In**.
10. A **From:** menu will appear where you will be asked to choose the location of your SmartThings.
11. Tick the checkbox corresponding to all the devices that Alexa will need to access.
12. Next, select the button **Authorize**.
13. A message will then appear, saying, "Alexa has been successfully linked with SmartThings."
14. Select the **x** icon to close the dialog window.
15. Alexa is now ready to discover (detect) devices.

Discovering Devices

What you just did in the process described above is to authorize Alexa to have access to the SmartThings devices you have. This is giving the Alexa app permission to discover (scan/detect) these devices and then you will be able to control them via voice control.

For Alexa to discover your SmartThings devices:

1. Right after closing the dialog box in the last step of the previous section (Connecting SmartThings), Alexa will automatically bring you to this section. The app will direct you to start discovering the SmartThings device/s.
2. Look for and tap the button **Discover Devices**.
3. Wait for a few seconds as Alexa discovers the SmartThings device/s that you input earlier.

In case you are not automatically prompted to discover the SmartThings device/s, you can do these steps:

1. Open the menu in the left navigation panel of Alexa app.
2. Select the option **Smart Home**.
3. Scroll down and select **Your Devices**.
4. In the menu that opens, select the option **Discover Devices**.
5. Wait for Alexa to discover your devices.

As Alexa discovers your SmartThings device/s, a progress bar is visible. It will take about 20 seconds for Alexa to discover the device/s you have authorized the app to access.

Once the process is complete, you should see the list of discovered devices in the section **Your Devices** of **Smart Home**.

You are now ready to use Alexa's voice control feature to control your SmartThings device/s.

You may start by trying requests such as these:

Alexa, turn off the kitchen lights.

Alexa, brighten the living room lights.

Alexa, raise the bedroom thermostat by 5 degrees.

Alexa, dim the bedroom lights.

Alexa, set the living room light to 7. (Brightness of lights can be adjusted within a range of 0 to 100.

Alexa, set the living room thermostat to 75 degrees.

Adding New Devices

You can keep adding SmartThings devices for Alexa to access and control via your Amazon Tap. You may also update or change the SmartThings devices. For example, if you added a new dimmer switch, a thermostat or an on/off switch, you will need to give Alexa access to these.

1. Open the menu, the one with the 3 horizontal lines.
2. Select the option **SmartApps**.
3. Choose the option **Amazon Tap**.
4. A list of devices that Alexa has current access to will appear.
5. Choose the option **My Thermostats** or **My Switches**.
6. Tick the checkbox of the devices that you want Alexa to have access to.
7. Select the button **Done**.
8. Choose the option **Next**.
9. Get you Amazon Tap and press the **Talk** button.
10. Make a request by saying, "Alexa, discover new devices."
11. Wait for a few seconds while Alexa finishes discovering new devices.
12. Alexa will notify you and confirm that the discovery has been completed.
13. Select the option **Done** once the confirmation is received.

Disconnecting SmartThings from Alexa

Performing this process will disconnect all your SmartThings devices from Alexa. When you give requests through Tap, Alexa will no longer be able to accept and respond to commands you give for these devices.

To disconnect using the SmartThings app:

1. Open the SmartThings app.
2. Select the menu from the left navigation panel, the one with the 3 horizontal lines.
3. Select the **SmartApps** option.
4. Choose the option **Amazon Tap**.
5. Select **Uninstall** option from the menu.
6. Tap the option **Remove**.
7. Confirm that you are removing the connection between SmartThings app and your Tap.

Next, disconnect SmartThings devices from your Alexa:

1. Select the menu from the left navigation panel (icon with 3 horizontal lines).
2. Select from the options **Smart Home**.
3. Scroll down the dropdown menu and tap the option **Your Smart Home Skills**.
4. Look for SmartThings and tap the **Disable** button beside it.
5. Confirm by tapping the button **Disable Skill**.

Conclusion

I hope this book was able to help you to understand and optimize your use of the Amazon Tap.

I wish you the best of luck!

To your success,

William Seals

www.ingramcontent.com/pod-product-compliance
Lightning Source LLC
Chambersburg PA
CBHW051212050326
40689CB00008B/1278